Uncommon Prayers

FOR YOUNG ADULTS AT WORK

Daniel Seagren

BAKER BOOK HOUSE
Grand Rapids, Michigan

To
LISA
and everyone in Sweden
who made our
three years together
so meaningful

Copyright 1978 by

Baker Book House Company

ISBN: 0-8010-8129-7

Printed in the United States of America

PREFACE

These prayers you are about to experience are neither orthodox nor unorthodox. They are somewhere in between. They are neither prose nor poetry; they are, perhaps, a little of each. But then, most prayers are not prose or poetry.

These prayers are candid portraits of young people grappling with the complexities of the workaday world. The speakers are Christians—strong and weak, salty and mild—slugging it out in the marketplace.

Most marketplaces, whether the equipment be a broom or a baton, are rough places for the committed young Christian—whether he or she knows it or not. At times the survival rate is alarmingly low. There is constant pressure to conform, to temporarily jettison a cumbersome, open faith.

That's why young pioneers and pilgrims at work need to pray—before breakfast, on the job, at noon, on the subway, or after work.

These prayers are not carefully rehearsed. They arise out of a need; they are desperate cries for help or spontaneous outbursts of gratitude. They remind us that at times God may seem far away but any believer can get His attention by throwing a prayer at His window.

That's what these people are doing. You may not recognize some of their occupations firsthand, but you'll quickly identify with their laughs and cries, their smiles and winces.

In these pages you'll meet many new friends. Pray with them—a couple of times, perhaps, and possibly aloud—and throw one of your own prayers at God's window. The Lord is there, and when you get His attention—it isn't difficult—you'll never regret it.

So . . . read on. And pray. You're among friends!

NOW I LAY ME DOWN TO SLEEP

Now I lay me down to sleep
  I pray the Lord my soul to keep.
  Keep me safely through the night
And wake me up at morning light.
Bless Mommy and Daddy and
all the missionaries.   A-men.

Remember, Lord, when
I prayed like this?

When was it I stopped praying
  If I should die before I wake
and used the more modern
  Keep me safely through the night?

When, Lord, did I stop praying?
  When I was unafraid of dying in my sleep?
  When I assumed I'd wake at morning light?
When did I outgrow my childhood prayer?
When did I outgrow prayer?

Somewhere . . . somehow
I put this childish prayer behind me.
On second thought, Lord,
it wasn't childish at all.
It had served me well.

I closed my eyes
I folded my hands
and slipped gently into dreamland.

But now I need You again, Lord—
yet how do I begin?

Now I lay me down to sleep
I know I'll improve within a week
Please wake me up at morning light
I'll need Your help to do what's right.

IF I SHOULD DIE BEFORE I WAKE

Death is heavy on my mind tonight:
Dorleen went to her grandfather's funeral
Denny was killed winding up his Porsche
Dawn just had an abortion
(but that's not quite the same—
or is it?)

I'm confused, Lord, and discouraged.
Maybe because it's three deaths in one week
Maybe it's because we don't think much about it—
at least not more than necessary.
But it is necessary.
I found out the painful way.

Dorleen's grandfather was old, very old—
perhaps he was happy to say good-bye

Denny was young, too young—
perhaps he was lucky he didn't survive

Dawn is so shallow, and immature—
perhaps it's better this way.

Tonight I feel so useless
like a tree stump
newly shorn of its
wisdom and grace.

I talked about the weather before I could
tell Dorleen how sorry I was

My hands trembled as I dialed Denny's house
to try to express my sorrow

I bit my lip as Dawn flippantly
dramatized her ordeal . . .

Long ago, Lord, I learned it well—
If I should die before I wake—
but what do I say or do
when someone else dies?

FOR THOSE WHO RUB ME THE WRONG WAY

Lord, some people
rub me the wrong way.
I've tried
but I can't help it.
I don't like them
I can't stand them
I won't tolerate them
and I certainly don't love them.
What can I do?

I hate to go to sleep
feeling this way.
Maybe if we talk about it
I'll feel better.

No matter what is done
Tom thinks he can do it better.
   Dick argues with everyone—just so he can hear
      himself talk.
Larry gloats in his pseudo superiority and
   Mary thinks she's God's gift
   to society. Poor Jane.
Jane thinks God passed her by and
   Sue is half child, half woman.
Tom, Dick and Larry . . .
Mary, Jane and Sue . . .
and me, grumpy, irritated me!

   Maybe
   I don't like them
   because I don't like me?

Well, not all of the time—
   sometimes I like me too much.

Anyway, Lord, I feel better
now that it's off my chest.
Thanks for listening . . . and
thanks for Tom, Dick and Larry, Mary, Jane and Sue.

I think I need them . . . might even like them.
Don't You?

O WHAT A BEAUTIFUL MORNING

Why can't every day
be like today?

   The sun was shining when I arose
   Breakfast never tasted better
   The 7:59 was right on time

So was the always-tardy professor
(and I aced his pop quiz)
Every library book I needed was in
No one raided my lunch bag
I got to work five minutes early
but the boss was sick so
I got the afternoon
off—with pay!

But why am I telling you all this, Lord?
You know what happened better than I.

O I'm sorry . . .
Did You say something?
I see . . .
Right.
Let's try it once again . . .

Thank You for waking me this morning
Thank You for letting the sun shine
Thank You for the chat on the 7:59
Thank You for the mind You have given me
Thank You for bacon 'n eggs 'n jelly sandwiches
Thank You for eyes good enough to read small
print
Thank You for thoughtful, generous people

Know something, Lord?

The day was even better
than I thought it was—
thanks to You.

VERDI ON WHEELS

You know about the writeup
in the paper today:

Singing Bus Driver Delivers
Arias and Passengers

Sure, I was pleased. Very pleased.

When I had failed one tryout after another
and had nowhere to go, I was bitter,
discouraged, frightened. What could a
voice major do without a singing job?

I could have taught,
but I don't like teaching.

I could have directed music,
but I'm not a conductor.

I could have gone to grad school,
but I was fed up with studying.

I could have switched majors,
but nothing else appealed to me.

That's when I looked You up again.

    We talked
    We probed
    We compromised. Remember?

I'm not sorry, Lord, really.
I love driving a bus and

my passengers don't seem to mind
a little Verdi or Mozart.

Maybe I'll drive the rest of my life.
Maybe not.
But whatever happens I can handle it,
thanks to You.

SAME PRAYER . . . DIFFERENT WORDS

Lord, why do You
keep on listening to me?
Every day I say the same old things.

Do You know how I know?
Last night I eavesdropped on myself
and didn't like what I heard.

It all began long ago when I was a kid.
I prayed every night before I went to sleep.
Then I entered high school
and someone said I'd never make it
if I didn't pray thirty minutes
every morning before I went to school.

I believed it. And I tried.
Believe me, it wasn't easy but
somehow I got my thirty minutes in.
Even though they were pretty mechanical,
I think they helped a little.

College came along
and I followed the same pattern.
Religiously. Mechanically.

Then graduation.
Interviews.
A job.
Not what I wanted, but a job.

Now the alarm interupts my sleep
and I grope for my robe as I
rub my eyes
and stumble to my knees
to mumble the same words again.

It's over, Lord. I smashed the record.

Now we can talk—together—
as we ought to do. Whenever we want to.
Or need to.

THANK YOU FOR NOT ANSWERING MY PRAYER

Oh, Lord, I'm exhausted so
only a couple of minutes tonight
but I must tell you what's happening.

Remember when I cried myself to sleep
because I didn't get the third grade
teaching job?

Well, all those tears were wasted.

Teaching kindergarten is
absolutely marvelous. Oh, I don't
mean it's easy because it isn't!

But such wonderful opportunities.

You remember Elisabeth . . .
such a little fuss-budget. I must
make sure she doesn't become an
incorrigible perfectionist.

And tough Erik. What a monster!
Somehow—and here I sure need Your
help—I must break his bullishness
without crushing his spirit.

Poor Eleanore. She gets far too much
of my time, but it's finally paying off.

Then there's little Erwin. So tiny,
timid, and terrified of every new
experience. His mother wants him to be
an astronaut, You know, but right now
he's scared to death of a swing.

Lord, I'm so happily exhausted I know
I will sleep well. Good night.

IT'S LONELY UP HERE

There was a time, Lord, when
I gave You all the credit
for what I had done.
In fact, we did it together:

> *magna cum laude*
> top two percent of the class
> fifty-seven interviews
> seventeen job offers
> highest starting salary
> fabulous fringe benefits . . .

Somewhere along the line
I forgot about You and began
to take most, then all, of the credit:

   successive salary increases
   increased responsibility
   bigger and more plush offices . . .

The higher I rose
the lower You fell.

Lord, I'm not in trouble
nor have I sinned grievously.
That's not why I'm looking You up again.

To be perfectly honest,
I'm lonesome.
It's lonely at the top. Terribly lonely.

But that's not all.
I'm lonely for You.

   If it's all right with You,
   I'd like to become friends again.

TO QUIT OR NOT TO QUIT

To quit or not to quit . . .
That is the question, Lord.

What do I do? It's getting worse.
   I've toned down my wardrobe
   I've unlisted my phone
   I've said no, No! NO!!
   but he won't give up.

Except for his compulsion, Lord,
he's a rather decent person:
    sensible
    efficient
    business-minded.
But horribly over-sexed.
I'm walking down a blind alley.

As long as I say no, no, no
I have no future—
    not with this firm
    not with this boss.

Lord, I've tried hard
to create a good image for the company
and to maintain my personal integrity
but I can't go on much longer like this.

What do I do?
What can I do?
What should I do?
    Blow the whistle on him?
    Hope that it'll blow over?
    Forget my security and quit?

Lord, the only reason I won't quit,
I guess, is that I'm afraid for my future.
But that's one of the fringe benefits
that comes from trusting You, isn't it?
Tomorrow he can start looking
for a new secretary. Praise the Lord!

A PROMISE IS A PROMISE

Wow, Lord. Can You imagine?
Me—a female DJ—with
50,000 watts at my disposal?

> Just think. I can spin
> these platters of gold
> as fast and as far
> as I want.

What an opportunity!
Somehow I've got to
manipulate the air waves—
that's the name of this game.

> We can take nobodies
> and transform them into
> folk heroes over night.

Incredible.
Diabolical, too.

I promised You—if I were chosen—
that I would spin Your name far and wide.
And I will.
> A promise is a promise!

Three Weeks Later

Uh, Lord, it isn't going so good.
I'm embarrassed.
And ashamed.

I'm, uh, taking orders—
not giving them.

I'm spinning platters and
ad libbing all right but I'm
getting my input from topside.

There's no room for You here, Lord.
We've got some great recordings
but the management takes a pretty
dim view of them. Anyway, Lord, I want
You to know that I'm down but not out.
Keep listening, Lord. I promised!

WHISPER A PRAYER AT NOON

Today on my lunch hour
I took my lazy bones
for a walk . . .
   mailed a couple of letters
   picked up *Newsweek* and *Time*
   soaked up a little mist
   which felt good after
   all this heat.

I walked past that little church
as I have dozens of times
but today I saw the marble madonna
for the very first time—
   her eyes sadly followed me
   as I drifted aimlessly by.

Why I stopped, Lord, I don't know
but these lazy bones turned
me around and led me
inside.

I was deeply moved
by the solitude which
swept over me, completely
drowning the noon hour rush.

I hardly noticed the old man
on his knees or the fragile little girl
in the last row—
I found myself kneeling
in the very front pew.

How long I lingered I do not know
but as I left I wondered
     why I hadn't done it before.
     Good night, Lord . . .
See You soon—at noon.

THOSE SANCTIMONIOUS FEW . . .

Something happened, Lord,
but I don't know when.
Or how.

You remember how I hated Sunday . . .
     those smug old ladies
     and sanctimonious men . . .
that wheezing organ which
drowned out the choir
(which of course was a blessing)
     those misplaced a-mens
     and stained-glass tears . . .

But then mercifully we moved up in the world,
found a church with a paid choir whose
cathedral tones pealed forth

18

no misplaced a-mens
piercing the air . . .

But there I thumbed through the hymnal,
counted bricks,
   prayed for shorter sermons
   and watched the clock.

So strange, I thought, to have a clock on the church
   wall . . .

But soon I was free
to do as I pleased
and took my leave . . .
   I worshiped outside in the great outdoors
   I replenished my soul in devious ways or simply
slept in late . . . if I stayed in town.

Now, much to my surprise but with no regret
I'm back in my favorite pew
   listening to a wheezy ol' organ
   and a misplaced a-men or two
   with no animosity toward those
   sanctimonious few.

P.S. Remember, Lord, when I didn't
believe in miracles?

THE DAY I GOT FIRED

Today I got fired, Lord,
and I'm torn apart inside.
No, not because I was fired
but because I deserved it.

I cut corners
I took advantage of people
I did sloppy work
I goofed off . . .
in fact, I was anything but Christian.

Even so, I had more integrity
than most of the others . . .

    they stole the company blind
    they undermined the boss
    they came late and left early
    they faked illnesses
    they padded their expenses
    they manipulated the books . . .

But that's not the point just now.
I really don't mind too much that
they have their jobs while I'm unemployed.

What is bothering me is that I
got away with it for such a long time.
It was humiliating to get caught, Lord,
not because the boss got wise
but because I didn't!

How could I live like that—
week after week—month after month?

Maybe getting fired was the best thing
that could have happened to me.
It's a pity it didn't happen sooner.

ECCLESIASTICAL ESPIONAGE

Lord, I need Your help,
not on this case particularly
but on my whole future.

You know how it all started:

    police academy
    promotion to officer
    detective assignment
    and now espionage.

At first I was honored. And flattered.

    I cherished the power
    I liked the fringe benefits
    I respected the cause . . .
but now I'm jittery.

    Not because my life is threatened
    Not because I distrust my government
    Not because I carry a gun
    Not because I travel incognito . . .
it's deeper than that.

    I'm forced to give evasive answers
    I deliberately feign friendships
    I avoid personal involvements
    I must sink only shallow roots
    I bend the truth if necessary . . .
and now I'm running scared.

I'm afraid to abandon my allegiance
to patriots without a conscience.

If I stay, would I be serving
Your best interests? And mine?
And those of my country?

Sometimes, Lord, it's simpler to live in limbo.
But can I live in limbo and serve You?
Or serve You well?

WHERE IN THE WORLD ARE YOU?

Where in the world are You
when I need You? Three times
yesterday I yelled for You . . .

How can I tell others how great You are
when You keep on ignoring me?

The guys at the office said,
"God is dead," which made me
madder than the devil.

And unless You do something
pretty quick I will think you're
deader than a doornail.

I'm no Elijah so I didn't call down
any fire but I did bet these characters
that my God is bigger than theirs.

I bet them that my God would
help me make a sales record this month.

That's why You've got to listen.
You can't afford to let me down because
it's a matter of life and death:

my life or Your death!
If I win, You win.
If I lose, You lose.

But don't worry. I'm not planning on losing
and I know You're not. You wouldn't be who You
are if You let me bully You around like this.

You know I always spout off
like this when I forget
who You really are.

It's been great talking to You
even if You probably
weren't paying
too much attention . . .

I THOUGHT I COULD HANDLE IT

I thought I could handle it, Lord
but now I'm not sure.
I was trying to prove that a Christian
could work as a hostess at this club
without playing their game.

This I can handle, Lord:
   anyone can fend off a man or two
   anyone can go straight home after work
   anyone can put lemon soda in a liquor glass
   anyone can *look* sexy without *being* sexy
   anyone can add and subtract . . .
that's all in a night's work.

It's the extras I can't seem to handle:
   unmercifully sizing up the big spenders
   listening continually to small talk

smiling sheepishly at cheap jokes
getting frustrated covering for the boss
watching the naive and gullible get taken
realizing how much time and money is wasted
night after night
week after week.

Lord, I think I have proved my point.
Six months have gone by
and I haven't begun to yield.

But something is going out
and nothing is coming in.
It's only a matter of time
before my soul will be empty.

Never before have I earned so much
and invested so little.

Lord, would You mind helping me
find a job that's bigger than I am
but just right for the two of us?

DON'T EVER TRUST A CHRISTIAN?

Lord, I know too much—
now I have serious doubts
about my ability to remain silent. I'm
all entangled with questions
about ethics.

It was much simpler
when I was a file clerk.
Even when I was a stenographer
I could do what I was told.
But now . . .

Lord, when does my loyalty
to my boss end? Is there any
chance that my loyalty to You
can conflict with my loyalty to him—
even though he is a Christian?

We aren't breaking the law—
only bending it a little.
   We aren't cheating our clients—
   only postponing their profits.
We aren't being dishonest—
only withholding certain facts.
   We aren't getting rich—
   we are simply guaranteeing our share.

Years ago, Lord, I wouldn't have done
what I am doing now. Can time alone
warp my better judgment or
condition my conscience?

   Why do I feel—no, not dirty—
   but somewhat soiled? Is it because
   I am—not impure—but tainted?
Lord, if our people cannot trust us,
whom can they trust?

UNSCRAMBLING SCRAMBLED EMOTIONS

Today while waiting
for an appointment
I thumbed through
some girlie magazines.
I thought I was relatively
   broadminded
   mature

sensible
shockproof
   but I guess I was wrong.

Lord, I had scrambled emotions
as I fed those pages into my mind . . .
   I thought of the girls 'n guys
   who bartered their endowments
   in the name of freedom
   for the sake of *art*—
   just because some voyeur
   needs vicarious gratification.

Then I thought of the publishers and editors
                    producers and photographers
                    printers and advertisers
before my mind wandered off again to the
   titillated teens and fascinated fanatics
   furious wives and frustrated males
which caused me to wonder
what would happen
if no one would pose
or no one would buy.

ON BEING PAID TO PRAY . . .

Lord, why is it I always
get asked to say the *blessing*?

Sure, I know we ministers are
supposed to know how to pray
but that doesn't mean that no one else
could ask the blessing on food.

Maybe I shouldn't resent it, Lord,
but I do. Do You know why?

26

It takes the honor away from
the host or hostess . . .

It insults the child who prays
when the minister does
it all over again . . .

It is a degrading courtesy
which implies an obligation
that it is my duty . . .

When I finished seminary I had
great visions of being some kind of
an ecclesiastical Galahad or spiritual Don Juan.
Now I see myself as some sort of a
Don Quixote (I never did fancy myself
a Saint Francis) . . .

But maybe I'm wrong.

Perhaps it's an honor for me to
say grace when I'm a guest . . .

Perhaps I *can* make a second blessing
without squelching a young innocent.

I suppose it is true: I am paid to pray.
That's infinitely better than
not praying at all, isn't it?

I DREAMED SWEET DREAMS

A year ago, Lord,
everything was secure—
  I knew what I wanted to be
  I took what I needed to take

I got what I needed to get
but now look at me:
   cum laude
   unemployed
   dejected.

What can I do with this worthless degree?
I loved chemistry but my heart
isn't in it any more!
   I can barely stand the
   sight and smell of a lab.
What's wrong with me?
What's wrong with the world?

I dreamed sweet dreams
but now life is nothing
but a nightmare.

Lord, what can I do?
   I cannot give up
   I dare not go back
   I must not start over ...

Can a chemist sell real estate
or an engineer design clothes?

I was ready to set the world on fire—
Now I can't even light a Bunsen burner.

I've heard it before
but is it true?
   Trust in the Lord ...
   He'll direct your paths.
Do You mean that, Lord?

If You do, You've got a semi-humbled
chemist who'll design clothes

or sell real estate or strike a light
if You want him to.

A SOPHISTICATED FACADE

God—
How'd I get into this mess?
How do I get out?
    I thought I had the
    perfect job . . . a job
    where I could show off
    and spite my parents
    at the same time.

You know, God, I never intended
to sell my body. No way. It's not
nor has it ever been for sale.

    That's what most seem to expect
    of a masseuse, though.

At first I thought this was
a high class establishment
but it turned out to be a
low class joint with a cheap
though impressive facade.

    Now I'm trapped.
    I've had my kicks
    I got my revenge
    I've impressed my friends
    and I've played it cool.

So, here I am: unsullied and unhappy!
Today I tried to talk seriously
with a client . . .

I told him I was a Christian.
He wouldn't believe it—or listen to me.

Finally, I evidently
got through to him—
he burst out:
   "What in the world are you doing here?"
That, God, is what I'm wondering, too.

MY JOB IS TOO BIG FOR ME

Lord, I can't possibly admit this
to anyone else except You.
   My job is too big for me
   and it's mostly my fault.

I cut too many corners . . .
I got better grades than I deserved . . .
I rode on the reputation of my school . . .
I was blessed with extremely competent secretaries.
   But now it has caught up with me.

I can't tell the directors . . .
I can't confide in the boss . . .
I can't share it with my colleagues
   and soon my subordinates will discover it
   (if they don't already know).

I toss and turn all night . . .
I'm nursing a nasty ulcer . . .
I'm nearly hooked on pills . . .
I work until late at night but I'm
   miserable
   guilty
   ashamed

incompetent
frustrated . . .

Lord, how do I go back down the ladder
I tried so desperately to climb?

I know every rung by name—
I have slivers from each one . . .

Would it be cowardly, Lord,
to throw away the old ladder
and start over again?

Or would it be heroic?

ONE SUNNYSIDE UP AND A PAIR SCRAMBLED EASY

Sometimes when I get home
I could scream.
Last night I did,
as You know.

I serve a *medium rare* and they
call it a burnt offering.
I serve a cup of coffee
and they mutter that it's
too hot or too cold.

But . . . just before I went to
work tonight I flipped on the TV
just to kill some time—or so I thought.
Now I'm wondering. . . .

There on the screen was an

interview with a foreign waiter
who was visiting our country.
Of course I had to listen.

One thing he said really impressed me.
He said that he was the middleman between
the chef and the customer. But more
than that, he said he was responsible
for seeing that the chef did what the
customer wanted. He said his job was to see
that the food looked nice and tasted good.

In fact, he actually tastes the food
before he serves it. I couldn't
believe it, Lord. I really couldn't.

But anyway, tonight I went to work
as the "go-between" between the chef and the
customers. I tried to be interested in what
they wanted and how they wanted it.
Then I made sure they got it. Attractively, too.

What a night it was and I don't mean the tips.

Tell me, Lord—did You have anything to do
with getting me to watch that TV interview?

THE NIGHT I ALMOST DIDN'T COME HOME

As You know well, Lord,
I almost didn't come home tonight.

   The weather was awful
   My car wouldn't start

Her roommate was gone and
no one would have known. . . .

When I went back to ring the bell
after fooling half an hour with
that stubborn ol' pile of bolts
    I was frustrated and angry—
    in need of some tender lovin' care.
What a set up!

She put the coffee pot on
    wiped the smudge from my face
    and the grease from my coat
    and teasingly cooed,
    "I hope your car will never start."
It didn't. Not tonight.

You know I tried to call
triple A, but at two a.m.
I ran out of (or into?) luck.

The last bus left at one and
she said I should stay since we both
are such responsible, mature adults.

I wanted to stay. Lord, You know
I didn't want to go home
to a cold, empty room.

    But that long walk in the cold
    turned out to be better
    than I thought.

Thanks, Lord, for keeping me company.

WHY DID I LET HIM GO AWAY?

Lord, why . . . why did I
let him go away?

   We're meant for each other—
   I know it, I know it, I know it!
But something always seems to go wrong . . .

I think he wanted to stay.
I wanted him to stay.
   We wouldn't have done anything wrong . . .
It would have been so cozy—
We could have talked all night.

   But no, off he goes
   into the black of night
   as though I had pushed him
   right out of my life.

But I didn't, Lord.
I had it all worked out . . .
It would have been so romantic.

   Wasn't it providential
   that his car broke down
   the same night
   my roommate left town?

What a perfect way to test our love.
But now he's gone and we
may never know just
how strong or weak . . .

   I suppose,Lord, I'll
   never see him again

but on the other hand
if he would have stayed
he might not want
to see me again.

Or I him.

WHEN THEY LAUGHED IN MY FACE

Lord, I've been hurt
and embarrassed
and now I'm not a little
ashamed.

We went out for lunch
to celebrate a birthday
with a little bit of class.

To rub it in, Lord,
because I took no gin
    They laughed in my face
    and asked me to say grace.

"You pagans," I muttered with regret,
"I'll teach you a lesson you'll never forget."

    I took a deep breath
    closed my eyes
    then opened my mouth and
    took 'em by surprise:

        Lord, as we bow,
        Thanks for the chow.

Now, I don't know why I said it, Lord.
    Were You angry?
    Embarrassed?

    Or weren't You listening?
You don't always listen
to everything we say
or take us too seriously,
do You?

But then, on the other hand,
if they hadn't asked me
to pray, would
that then have meant
they didn't know
I could?

    Maybe I was embarrassed for nothing . . .

MOTHER NATURE AND FATHER GOD

We have some marvelous scapegoats.
Whenever we cannot find a cause
or a solution we can blame
Mother Nature and Father God.

Lord, we have a terrible time
differentiating between the problems
of nature and our own
destruction of the environment.

Who should be blamed when
    rivers run wild
    rains refuse to fall
    earth heaves and buckles
    air refuses any more impurities
    pesticides seep into water
    sludge fouls the beaches
    species verge on extinction
    oil and forests vanish . . . ?

I try to remind my scientific colleagues
that we have no right to blame our woes
on Father God and Mother Nature simply because
we cannot or will not solve our ecological riddles!

When I argue that we pollute the air
and ravage the elements, they agree.
But then they strike back and hit me with the
multiple curses of famine, flood and pestilence.

   I love the earth, the sun, moon and stars
   I love the bounding seas and babbling brooks
   I love the mountains, deserts and plains
   I love cozy villages and frantic cities . . .

But I love You too much
to let You get blamed where You are blameless.

You gave us a mighty fine place to live.
Now we need Your help to keep it that way.

MY GOD, MY GOD,
WHAT HAVE I DONE?

Oh, my God, what do I do now?
   I know what I ought to do
   but it's not what I want to do!
That's my problem.
And now it's Yours too.

I didn't want it to happen
and I tried to not let it happen:
   we fell in love (which is exhilarating)
   but she is married (which is exasperating).

It all began when we were assigned
to a special project which threw us
close together.
We both fought it—at first—
but now the vibrations are overwhelming.

God, what do I do?

She wants a divorce
so we can make it legal—
and moral . . .
    but would it ever be morally right?

Now I can see how subtle and swift
flow the passions of the innocent
(and those not so innocent) . . .
    I was lonely and she was unhappy
    I flirted a little and she responded
    I was teasing but she was serious
    I was vulnerable and . . .

My God, oh, my God, what have I done?

    I know what I ought to do
    but I don't think I can
    do it alone . . .

    That's why I came back . . .
    if it's not too late.

COFFEE, TEA, OR SYMPATHY?

Did I ever thank You, Lord,
for helping me land this position?
I meant to but don't think I did . . .

That was seven years ago
and I have flown high and wide
since then. Mostly wide.

I prayed then—oh how I prayed
that You'd help me—remember?

Now I'm twenty-eight with little more
than memories and some seniority.

But my prospects appear, unfortunately,
to be pretty meagre. It's sad, but true!

I feel guilty and not a little ashamed
coming to You now after all these years:
    routine is displacing intrigue
    boredom is overtaking excitement
    hope is fading into nonchalance
    restraint is replacing yearning . . .

I'm still flying high
but discovering
surely but slowly that
    tending bar
    serving meals
    selling cologne
    and tobacco
is flying just a little too low.

I'm sorry to bother You, Lord,
after this long absence
    but I'd like to fly higher
    except I don't think I can.

    Unless I fly with You.

ONCE UPON A TIME A BRICKLAYER . . .

Remember the story
about the two bricklayers who
were asked what they were doing?

One said he was making a wall,
the other said he was building
a cathedral . . .

Well, Lord, I've been laying
bricks for five years. No wonder my job
is boring, hard, and discouraging.

We work in the rain and snow . . .
We work in blistering heat and in
              unbelievable wind-chills . . .

We yell for more *mud* . . .
We plead for better *mud* . . .
We reject impossible *mud* . . .

   Lord, I'm glad I heard about those
   two bricklayers—too bad I
   didn't hear about them five years ago.

I'm still yelling for more *mud* and better *mud*
My walls are no straighter
My fireplaces don't work any better.
But I'm not merely laying bricks any more—

   I'm building houses and
   creating beautiful fireplaces
   and erecting high rises and
   making safe edifices which can

argue eyeball to eyeball with an
earthquake . . .

Ever since I quit laying bricks and
started building cathedrals
my whole outlook on life
has changed.

Lord, I feel so good about it
I just had to tell You.

PEONS, DRUDGES, AND ROBOTS

Today I fell asleep on the job.
I was embarrassed
  reprimanded
  laughed at . . .
No, I wasn't tired. Just bored.

Lord, is this all there is to life?
Must I twist valves and read gauges
until rigor mortis sets in?

I don't know what to do.
Someone's got to adjust these valves,
read the temperatures and release
the pressure so that the building
is reasonably liveable.
And safe.

I guess I deserved to be scolded.
I had no business falling asleep
even if there is an automatic
warning system built in . . .

  Lord, I just object to being depersonalized
    I am not a machine or a robot

I am not a drudge or a peon
I am a person—even if I am
handicapped.

I know, the pay is good and I have a lot
of energy left over at the end of the day.

That's why I'm a scout leader,
volunteer custodian, bus driver
and you-name-it for our youth groups.

So far, that's what has kept me going
but I'm not sure I can hang in there
for the next thirty years.

Do You suppose—maybe—that I
should retrain for something else?

I don't have the nerve, Lord.
That's why I'm mentioning it to You.

S-E-C-U-R-I-T-Y

Security.
I hate the sound
of the word, Lord,
because it has chained
me to a post and I don't dare to
break away . . .

I like my work.
The pay is tops.
The fringe benefits are good
and the raises
are automatic.

I can come and go as I please,
take time off when I want,
schedule my own vacations
and almost name my own terms.

That's the trouble, Lord.
I'm suffocating under all
this security. I have it so good
I have lost nearly all my incentive:

my creativity has suffered
my courage is non-existent
my goals are small
my ambition is diminishing . . .

I'd be a fool to start over
from the bottom, but that's exactly
what I ought to do.

I must be creative
I must take risks
I must set higher goals
I must drive myself
  or I shall die!

Lord, please . . .
please don't let me die.

THE DAY I CRACKED THE SEX BARRIER

Ah, yes, I was so proud
when I cracked the sex barrier . . .

Women had been ignored
              avoided
              discriminated against

and underestimated
far too long!

I fought hard for this position.
I worked hard to prove my competence.
I prayed hard for the needed strength.

Now I want to thank You, Lord.
It was worth the struggle
(although it isn't over yet).

I didn't do it only for myself.
I did it for all women—everywhere.

We've got a foot in the door . . .
We've got lobbyists everywhere . . .
We've got equal pay (just about) and
equal rights (almost).

So, here I sit, Lord, on top
after ten long, lonely years.

But now what? What's next?
I've proved my point . . .
I've mastered the business . . .
I've earned deep respect . . .
I've fulfilled my ambition.

It was great
struggling against overwhelming odds
but now that the odds favor me
I find far less fulfillment
in simply maintaining
what I've already earned.

Lord, how do I fight these odds?

IS IT A SIN TO SWITCH?

Remember, Lord, when I struggled
to get the hang of calculus?
Now I'm an engineer but . . .

Here I am, saddled with a pleasant desk job
         solving riddles with a calculator
         snarling at careless draftsmen
         sitting on endless committees . . .

Lord, I'm not terribly bored
nor am I incompetent.
I can handle most any assignment
although I don't always like it.

But . . .
Today I had my car tuned.
It cost a small fortune
but what was worse
it ran terribly.

I was disgusted and angry.
That's when it happened.
I decided to retune it myself.

Tonight as I was working on my car
—in spite of my resentments—
I thoroughly enjoyed it:

   the chilly, moist evening air
   the smell of grease on my hands
   the one skinned knuckle
   and the inner satisfaction when that engine
      purred like a kitten . . .

Lord, would it be a sin
to switch from being a
second-rate engineer to a
first-rate mechanic?

ISN'T THAT A MAN'S JOB?

Lord, ever since I took this job
I've been branded everything from
effeminate to gay . . .
You know, Lord—how well You know—
I'm not a homosexual.

It's a tragedy what people think—
not for me but for them.

  I just happen to enjoy home economics
  I know I can outcook many women
  I know it isn't much help when people
  discover that I design my own clothes . . .

Lord, why is it I could be
a master chef and be praised
but cursed because I
teach kids to cook?

I won't quit—no matter what.
I find much more satisfaction
in the classroom than in the kitchen.

Another matter. I'm doing a little moonlighting.
I've agreed to run the church nursery on weekends.
  That shook up a few smug saints
  but it does rescue a few of these
  little ones from their feminine domination.
  That isn't all bad, is it?

One more thing.
Lord, I need Your advice.
They want me to revamp the church
PA system. Should I?

Or isn't that a man's job?

THANK YOU, LORD, FOR LITTLE PEOPLE

Tonight I don't feel
nine feet tall—
    and I don't want to.

I like my size
I like my sex
I want to be me.

    My IQ is just right, Lord—
    not too great and not too small

    My nose is just right, too—
    not too big and not too puny.

I will never set the world on fire
but neither will I fiddle while it burns.

I will never be famous or rich
but I am content to be what I am.

    I will always be average
    but never middle-of-the-road.

    I may be fooled sometimes and even naive
    but I'm not foolish or stupid.

I'll always have more to do than time will allow
but I'll never be bored.

The burdens might get heavy, Lord,
but never greater than I can bear.

When the whistle blows
I can go home and when the
exam is over
I can live with a C.

When I look at a woman
I'm glad I'm a man
and when I think of sex
I don't mind a little wait.

Thank You, Lord, for making little people--
like me.

IS THE CUSTOMER ALWAYS RIGHT?

Some days are worse than others
but this was incredible:

I was insulted repeatedly
I was called an outright liar twice
I missed my coffee break thanks to a supersnob
I got bawled out (needlessly) by the manager
I argued back (which I shouldn't have)
I fouled up the cash register twice
I forgot to return a couple of credit cards
I failed to sign a refund form . . .

But that's enough for my problems.
Some of them I deserved but
the others were unearned.

Lord, is the customer always right?
Should they be privileged people?

We are taught to smile sweetly
no matter what happens. Lord,
sometimes I just can't do it. I really can't:

> not when I have a splitting headache
> not when the customer is downright rude
> not when some idiot ruins my lunch hour
> not when a two-bit manager throws his weight
>
> not when a customer comes in at closing time . . .

If I were an angel I could probably hack it
but I'm not. And You and I both know it.

But it still bothers me every time I zap someone
and I do feel awfully good when I smile through
   my tears.

You know, I skipped breakfast today.
I skipped talking to You, too.
I suppose the two together
sort of ganged up on me.

Tomorrow I'll chat with You
as I scramble my egg and sip coffee.

Maybe then the customer will be right.

ON TOUCHING EVERY BASE

At first, Lord, it was great sport—
that's when it was a sport.
But now it's business . . . big business!

We play only to win
We learn to get psyched-up
We hire agents and join unions
We get traded like cattle
We live under fierce pressure

Now I must make a decision
but it would be so much easier
if someone would make it for me.

(I couldn't keep my mind on the game today,
so the manager sent me to the showers.)

My alma mater wants me to return
as head coach. What do You think?

I'd be trading a pitcher's mound
and half my salary for a little more
security and deeper roots.
Is that a bargain
or am I kidding myself?

Would I play only to win?
Would we buy and sell?
Would I dash hopes and break spirits?

What if we had a losing season?
What would the fans do?
Would the alumni understand?
Would the pressure be any less?

Lord, pressure is the name of the game.
That's why I need Your help.

I have two more weeks to decide.
Would You mind helping me touch all the bases?
Then I'll get home safely.

BEYOND THE CALL OF DUTY

What an experience!

Three months now I've been
apprenticed to pots 'n pans.
Soon I'll be making beds
and scrubbing toilets.

But I had to do it!

If I'm going to work with immigrants
I've got to go where they are
do what they do
feel like they feel
think as they do . . .

These people are strangers in a strange land.

They don't speak our language
They don't know our customs
They are bewildered and confused
They are excited with great expectations
They are naturalized citizens and illegal aliens
They are political refugees and malcontents
They are poverty-stricken and highly
sophisticated
They are lazy and hard-working
They are religious and irreligious . . .

Some will adjust—others cannot.

Some will scrub pots and pans forever
while others will someday own the restaurant.

Lord, make me sensitive
to their situation
without either
paternalism or
condescension.

Above all, help them see
that You love them—
through me.

IT IS LONELY IN A CROWD

I see it now but why couldn't
I see it before, Lord?

Do we always have to find out the hard way?
Must we always hurt someone before we learn?
Are we born stubborn?

Five years I have lived in the city.
Five years have been wasted—
well, make that four . . .

I've heard it said that "you can take
the boy out of the country but you
can't take the country out of the boy."

Now I believe it.
But what can I do?

If I go home my father will never let me forget it.
If I don't go home, I will never forgive myself.

Lord, I never thought I would yearn again

for a rooster crowing at five
for the smell of new-mown hay
for the sight of a newborn colt
for the beauty of a harvest moon
for the long-range weather forecasts . . .

Here it doesn't matter if it rains or not
it is impossible to smell the hay
it is difficult to see the stars
it is lonely in a crowd . . .

Lord, I'm no city slicker.
I'm a farmer and I know it.

Lord, if You'll help me swallow my pride,
I'll go home where I belong.

I might . . . yeh, I might even
be wrong about my father.
He might be happy to have me back.

WANDA THE WELDER

When I first started to work
they called me Rosie the Riveter.
Now they call me Wanda the Welder
but it really doesn't bother me.

Today the big boss came by
to inspect our work
(I was welding gas pipe today).
He found no leaks, which
quickly shut some loud mouths.

Lord, I'm not sure why I tackle these jobs.
First I learned to drive a truck

Then it was pumping gas
Now I'm welding six-inch pipes . . .
No, I'm not out to prove anything
(at least I don't think I am).
I'm just taking advantage
of being free as a bird.

Lord, until You introduce me
to the right man (I don't seem to
be managing it by myself) I'm going
to keep on enjoying my freedom.

Then—if and when—I'll
gladly settle down . . .

Know what I did today?
I sent for an application
to scuba diving school.

Why not live in the best of both worlds?
I can weld up here in the summer
and scuba dive—professionally—
the rest of the time. Maybe I can
land one of those salvage jobs.

Besides, I might meet a Prince Charming
somewhere along the way.
It could be arranged,
couldn't it?

JOIN THE NAVY AND SEE THE WORLD

I joined the Navy and guess what I saw:

dirty dungarees and unpolished boots

obstacle courses and thirty-second haircuts
pots and pans, mops and buckets . . .

Then bootcamp was over and I saw some more:

bilges and bulkheads
hatchcovers and booms
diesels and evaporators . . .

Then it slowly dawned on me that I
actually was seeing the world—
a miniature world of its own with

liberties and libertines
language I had hardly imagined
loneliness and homesickness

I don't know what I expected
but it wasn't what I experienced.

I dreamed of exotic islands and hula girls
I dreamed of Hong Kong and Rio
I dreamed of balmy seas and misty sunsets . . .

I was a great romantic, Lord—
half man and half boy.

But I did see the world—
at its best and at its worst.

I've weathered the storms and now I'll be

better and wiser
stronger and smarter
braver and more cautious . . .

I've seen the world, Lord—
it's pretty rough out there.

That's why I'm not going back into it alone.
This time we'll tame those seas—together.

LORD, IF THERE'S ANOTHER WAY . . .

Whose idea was it that I
should become a policewoman?
Mine? Or Yours?

But why? Altruism?
            Patriotism?
            Maternalism?

That's what's getting to me, Lord.

I never believed in a maternal
instinct before—not until
I began to mother these girls.

I need help. Badly. Soon.

I know we aren't supposed to get
emotionally involved or
bring our work home with us.

    That's okay on paper . . .

These poor kids . . .
    oversexed
    undernourished
    hyperemotional . . .
        feisty but fragile
        feminine but frustrated

foolish but frolicsome
frightened but flippant . . .

As You know, I have three parolees
living in my apartment. I know
that probably
could cost me my job.

Really, these girls don't need me.
They need You. But I can't tell them
that on the job . . .

Lord, if there's another way—
or a better way—I'm listening.

BYPASSED AGAIN!

Lord, again I was left off the list.
I'm struggling but I'm afraid
it's a losing battle.

Is it because I lack competence?
Is it because I am not diplomatic?
Is it because my faith gets in the way?

If I only knew . . .

I vowed that my faith would never
be compromised on the job or elsewhere.
Now I'm beginning to wonder if it pays off:

I've turned the other cheek
I've lent a helping hand
I've gone the second mile
I've witnessed discreetly

I've tried, tried, tried
but I'm getting weary of trying!

Yes, I know we are not supposed to get weary
in well-doing but that's exactly
what is happening.

Is it unnatural to want fairness?
Is it wrong to want recognition?
Is it presumptuous to expect a promotion?

Is that asking too much?

If I only knew, Lord, if I am
really incompetent or tactless
or if my faith comes on too strong
or if it is a combination of things.
Or none of these. How can I know?

Shall I wait longer or quit now?
Shall I subdue my faith or intensify it?
Shall I try harder or not so hard?

Whatever You say, Lord, I'm listening . . .

EXTERNAL BEAUTY AND INNER LOVELINESS

Lord, I have helped hundreds of women—
or I would like to think I have.

At first it was fascinating
to study their features
in order to accentuate the lovely
and diminish the unattractive.

To some extent it worked wonders.

Today a woman came in but I couldn't help her.

Her features were utterly impossible.
Her eyes were absolutely unresponsive.
Her hair had been destroyed long ago.

After an hour I nearly gave up.

As I labored—and I mean labored—
she talked. And the more she talked
the more she came alive. What a
marvelous person she was!
She had a faith You wouldn't believe (on second
thought I think You would) . . .

When I made the finishing touches
I was ashamed at my obvious failure.

I stood back and inspected my craftmanship.
Her eyeshadow was wrong but her eyes had
come alive and it didn't matter.

Suddenly, it dawned on me.
Her beauty came from within.
No wonder I couldn't improve it—
or damage it.

I learned a lesson today, Lord.

From now on, please help me
not to become so preoccupied with external beauty
that I overlook the loveliness which comes
from within.

WANTED: A SENIOR PARTNER

Almighty God, our dear heavenly Father.
We come now into Thy holy presence . . .

O Lord, my God . . .
I can't pray like that
but I don't know any other way.

It's been a long time and all
I can remember is how my
grandfather prayed.

He was a real saint
and although his prayers sounded
much too solemn to suit me
there is no doubt where they went.

I'm third generation in this
family business. Soon dad will
step aside and the responsibility
will rest on my shoulders.

Grandpa had no education.
Dad went through the ninth grade.
I am a university graduate
    but I feel so inadequate.

Our business has expanded considerably . . .
The unions have incredible powers . . .
Employees know their rights (which is good)
and often exploit them (which is bad).

Lord, the era of a simple family enterprise
has been invaded by inflation,

sophisticated extortion, and is entangled in
miles and miles of red tape.

Grandfather never saw it coming.
Father watched it develop and
I have it right in my lap!
   And I don't even know how to pray.

I need a partner. A Senior Partner, Lord.
Would you like to join the firm—again?

MISPLACED HERO WORSHIP

Father, forgive them
for they know not what they do.
I'm not being sarcastic
or sacrilegious, Lord, but I find
it difficult to forgive . . .

We played another concert tonight
and the crowd went crazy.
Absolutely wild.

At first I ate it up . . .
Then it went to my head . . .
Now I'm embarrassed. Awfully embarrassed.

We're not that good, Lord.
Tommy, Benje, Fritz, Murph
and Rudi know it too but
   we have a shrewd promoter
   we lucked out on TV
   we pulled a few strings and, yeah,
   we probably do have some talent.

But why should people worship us?
Why do we let them? Or encourage it?

We don't deserve to be worshiped.
　It isn't healthy
　It isn't right
　It isn't going to last, either.

One of these days the bubble will burst.
Then what? If we can't handle the applause now
what'll we do when it stops?

Lord, these people know not what
they are doing to us.
How can I forgive them?
How can I forgive myself for
letting them do this to me—
　especially when I know better?

LORD, GET ME OUT OF HERE!

Lord, You've got to get me out of here.

　Three weeks and I've
　gained twelve pounds.

　I know, I told You I'd do anything
　if You'd only help me find a job.

　But in a bakery?

I can't resist, Lord. I simply can't.

They told me I'd stuff myself
for a week or so but after that I could

62

look a cream puff in the eye and tell it
to drop dead.

Nonsense! All day long,
day after day, I nibble
on cookies and pick up crumbs
(can't seem to waste 'em) . . .

I keep on telling myself that it can't
or won't continue. But look at me!
Every day a new bulge in a new place.

Lord, I really appreciate all the help
You gave me when I came begging.

But now I have second thoughts.
Maybe I chose this job, not You . . .
How can I be sure?

On the other hand, you know how
weak my resistance is to most anything.
Perhaps You put me here for a purpose . . .

Wouldn't it be great, Lord, if I could conquer
my appetite and develop self-discipline—
all at the same time?

Let's try one more week, okay?

YOU CALL THIS PHOTOGRAPHY?

You know, Lord, it started as a hobby.

I inherited a broken-down old
box camera and now I make my
living shooting pictures.

And I love it. Oh, how I love my work.

Portraits and weddings
Emergencies and front page events
Exotic countries and, ah, beautiful women

There's the snag, Lord, beautiful women!

Today I locked the shutter
on my camera and went home.

I should have known better
but I didn't read the small print
of my contract
(I seldom do).

This assignment wasn't photography today.

It was exhibitionism   (creative art said they)
which bordered somewhere between
poor taste and vulgarity.

I'm hardly a prude—You know that, Lord—
but today I refused.
Absolutely.
Unconditionally.

I know they'll sue for
breach of contract.
But no matter. I'm not worried.

I'd much rather accept this fate
than to see my camera degrade one of
the most photogenic subjects
You ever designed.

SECOND THOUGHTS ABOUT CONFIDENTIALITY

I'm going to miss this job, Lord.

It hardly seems possible that
seven years ago I came to help out
a little and have been here ever since.

    At first it was cutting stencils
    and running the bulletin . . .

    This was followed by answering the
    telephone and diverting cranks
    and busybodies . . .

    Then I was taking dictation which
    went fine as long as the pastor didn't
    use too many strange words . . .

Soon it was rather normal routine
as each day fell into its proper perspective.

Well, anyway, You know how it went.

Gradually it became more difficult.
Not the work. The pressure.

As the pastor developed more and more
trust in me, he confided more.
At first certain letters he
would type himself, but gradually he turned
those over to me. Before long I knew
far more than I wanted to know . . .

I was pleased that he trusted me
but scared to death that someday
something would spill out . . .

Now, Lord, as I leave this position
to marry another pastor,
help me—please help me to be understanding
when my husband withholds confidential
information from me. It may not be easy,
but I want to be his wife,
not his secretary.

WHAT IF I MESSED UP?

Some days, Lord, I don't see nobody
from midnight on. It sure gets
quiet—only me and them boilers—
and You. I know You're here, Lord,
even though I can't see You.

You know what I do. It ain't too hard
except sometimes it gets kinda hot
in here. All I gotta do is shovel the
coal in, take them clinkers out, and
keep turning them valves so nothing explodes.

Sometimes I wonder, Lord, what would happen
if I messed up. For sure I know I'd go
flying and so would a lot of other people.
That keeps me going, Lord.

The other people depend
on me. I can't let them down, can I?
I can't let nobody down.

That just ain't right, is it?
Maybe my job isn't too important

compared to a lot of other people—but I
think it's important. That's why I work,
even if I ain't feeling so hot—like now.

You know, Lord, I think I feel
a little better just knowing You
are here listening to me. You
and me do a pretty good job together,
don't we?

EX-CHAIRPERSON

You know my father,
so you must know why I hate men!
    I can't forgive him
    I don't even want to try
I don't want to call You "Father," either

Yes, Lord, I am bitter
I've never told You this before
In fact, I've never told anyone.

Being Chairperson of the
League of Lonely Lesbians
is getting me down, Lord . . .
    I hate making a living
    by propagating something
    I inwardly despise but
    outwardly espouse.

For years I couldn't—
    or wouldn't—
talk with You because You are male
and I totally rejected

a masculine deity.
But now I only hate him, not You.

Is it true that You won't forgive me
unless I forgive him? If so, I'll try
because I can't go on hating men
simply because . . .

Father, forgive me
as I forgive my father . . .
and deliver me from evil. Amen.

THE OTHER SIDE OF THE BAR

Just when alcohol conquered me
I'm not sure, Lord . . .

I attended seminars
I joined clubs
I tried dehydrating institutes
and hospitals and mental houses . . .

One day (strangely enough) I felt the urge
to visit a minister and so I went—fully
expecting to get thrown out . . .
or, perhaps get a powerful lecture.
Believe it or not, he did neither.
He must be one of Your better men, Lord.

After several long talks
some walks in the woods and
a couple of ball games

he showed me an ad from the local newspaper:

Wanted: Experienced Bartender

I almost laughed at his little joke
until I realized it was no joke.
At his urging I applied
(all my experience was on the wrong side
of the bar) and they hired me.

Later, Lord, I realized he was not only
trying to rehabilitate me but he was trying
to crack that establishment, too.

For six months I haven't touched a drop . . .

I listen to those who need to talk
I weep with those who want to weep
I talk to those who want to listen—and
I pray with those who ask to pray.

This may not last much longer, Lord,
because the bar is getting a reputation—
but I'm willing to stay until either
You or the boss tells me to go. Amen, Lord.

ON TEACHING (AND USING)
PLAIN ENGLISH

Lord, I am delighted with my
teaching position, Lord. It is
everything, Lord, I could have wanted.

These prepositions and verbs, Lord,
are challenging to teach, to say nothing,
Lord, about split infinitives,
Indo-European Roots, and anachronisms, Lord.

Lord, I find it difficult to get
as excited with the teaching of
spelling, Lord, but perhaps, Lord,
one of these days . . .

Creative writing is another subject,
Lord, that I thoroughly enjoy. To watch
these youngsters come alive, Lord, as
they create ideas out of words, is a
delight, Lord. Lord, You know what I mean,
don't You, Lord?

Excuse me a moment, Lord. I hear the telephone.
I'll be just a moment, Lord.

I'm back again, and am I embarrassed.
No, *chagrin* is a much better word.

I left the tape recorder
on and accidently recorded the first
part of our conversation. I was stunned,
dumbfounded. . . . It was deplorable!

I know so much better. How could I?
Please, please forgive me, Lord.

Our Father . . . hallowed be thy name . . .
Beware of vain babblings and meaningless
  repetitions . . .

From now on I'll mend my own language.

THE TICKET-TAKER GOT TAKEN

When I decided to moonlight
I didn't need the money—
I only thought I did.

But now I do!
It's a pity but true.

At first I did weekend matinees
which wasn't bad at all (I only
goofed around Sunday afternoons anyway).

These were the kid shows and I
didn't mind leading a five-year-old
to the restroom or helping find a
quarter dropped under a seat.

But then I inherited the night shift.
I didn't know what I was inheriting, Lord.

This cinema is schizophrenic I'm afraid:

charming fairylands by day
chilling violence and sex by night.

Frankly, Lord, I am embarrassed
by what is shown and more so
because I am showing the way.

The easy way out, I suppose, would be to quit.

I can readjust in time but it
won't be easy.
I'm hooked on a double income.

But I suppose I will quit anyway.

What bothers me, Lord, is not only what is
going on in the name of entertainment
but how deceptively naive I was.

Lord, forgive me for my
unworldly naivety.

A RHAPSODY OF CLICHÉS

Pumping gas is a lot of fun
especially when working in the sun . . .

> but in a driving rain
> or after dark when faced
> by a gun it isn't nearly
> as much fun.

But—there are worse things, Lord.

We're taught to chisel and cheat . . .
The boss says—

> "put the dipstick in part way"
> "slash the fanbelt so it shows"
> "exploit normal tire cracks"
> "wriggle those perfectly good balljoints"
> "sell 'em all kinds of junk . . ."

Lord, I can't do it . . .
I just can't!

> It turns my stomach
> It grates my nerves
> It keeps me awake nights

I need this job, Lord
You know I do,
but what do we do now?

  Keep fakin' the boss out?
  Ignore his dishonest instructions?
  Pretend like an actor?
  Tell him to go jump?

Lord, it's not only the matter of the job.
I could quit and find another
but this jerk would keep on
chiseling and cheating his
way into the black.

  I can't let him do that, Lord.
  I know I must stop him
  but I don't know when, where or how!

Do we eyeball him tonight, Lord?

MS.

Lord, it's great sport
going incognito!
  People don't know if I'm married
  or fifty or a swingin' single.
But why am I telling You all this?

Anyway, I've discovered that
signing my manuscripts Ms.
isn't as anonymous as I thought.
  Every editor knows I'm a woman
  which may or may not
  be to my advantage . . .
So now I simply use my initials

and let them guess.
    B. K. could go both ways,
    couldn't it?

Something, I guess, is bothering me—
or I wouldn't be telling You these things.

    Lord, I'm proud of my sex
    I'm not resentful or envious
        or bitter
        and I want to keep it that way.
    I don't even think editors
    give two hoots if I'm female or male
    if they like or need what I write.

Today I guess I'll have to confess
that I was upset when I received a
rejection slip addressed *Mr. B. K.*
I wonder if I would have been
equally distressed if it would
have been a check!

    Here I am, Lord: Ms. Mr. B.K. or whatever!
    From now on just call me Bernice.
    I think I like that best.

SNOB OF THE MONTH

I thank You, Lord, that I am not like these other
people:

    I get to the office on time
    I am never late with my rent
    I never miss my Rotary luncheons
    I tithe on the net of all I earn
    I seldom miss church . . .

I keep an immaculate apartment
I date but don't mess around
I respect the privacy of others
I give away old clothes and used books
I hate sin but love sinners . . .

Perhaps that's why I'm getting ahead in the world!
Thank You, Lord, that I am not like these other
people:

They never arrive on time
Their bills are always overdue
They disregard their obligations
They merely give a buck now and then
They rarely attend church

They live in unbelievable untidiness
They're always messing around
They are oblivious to solitude
Their stinginess is wretched . . .

Last week, Lord, I was elected SNOB OF THE
MONTH but that doesn't bother me. These people
in the office are jealous as You understand—
their pettiness is so cheap!

I find it so disconcerting
that no one ever listens to me
when I tell them about You.

I had dreams, Lord, of witnessing
the conversion of every member of the firm—
from the custodian up.

Perhaps, Lord, You know what went wrong?

THE BALLAD OF A BROOM

Nobody nowadays knows what to call us:
  domestics?
  maids?
  servants?
  cleaning ladies?
  dust dispensers (D. D.)?

I don't really mind too much, really, Lord.
You know why? Because I'm happy. And when I'm
happy I sing and when I sing everyone is happy.

Yesterday I made up a new song.
I wasn't treated very good and so
is was hard to sing—or smile.
But I thought I better sing anyhow
even if I didn't feel like it.
Want to hear how it goes?

The Ballad of a Broom

Once upon a time I was feelin' blue—
Lordy Lord, I didn't know what to do
  So I grabbed my broom and held on tight
  The dust went a flyin' left and right.

My boss and his lady are sometimes mean—
I scrub and I scrub but it's never clean
  So I grabbed my broom and held on tight
  The dust went a flyin' left and right.

Evil thoughts arise so I shut my eyes—
I pray the Lord as I look to the skies

So I grabbed my broom and held on tight
The dust went a flyin' left and right.

One of these days I'll simply disappear—
I'll ride my broom right out of here
So I grabbed my broom and held on tight
The dust went a flyin' left and right.

Lord, You know I wouldn't do that
but I just thought You'd like to know
how I feel some days . . .

THE BEST THAT MONEY CAN'T BUY

When I was a boy I was fascinated
with uniforms . . . and like most
little boys I wanted to be
  a fireman
  a policeman
  an army officer
  a chauffeur . . .
and so I became a cop.

Simple, wasn't it, Lord?

I enjoy it . . . it is fascinating:

  I've got my uniform
  I wear a gun (but never use it).

But I think I overestimated the job
or perhaps I underestimated myself.

  The uniform has lost its fascination
  The gun has lost its authority
  The routine has lost its novelty.

Yes, Lord, I'm just as fascinated as ever
but my task is completely unpredictable.

    I'm thrown into the middle of
    family squabbles but I'm not a
    social worker . . .

    I risk my life just to rescue a cat
    or unlock a jammed door . . .

    I am not a father confessor or a
    big brother, a statistician
    or a private eye. And I do not wink easily.

Lord, it would be much simpler to blow a whistle
at Fifth and Main but I'd rather smash payoffs
and help eradicate graft . . .

I'm glad I'm a cop but I
want to be the best that money can't buy!

YOU SHOULD HAVE SEEN THEIR FACES!

Lord, You should have seen their faces
when I served Holy Communion.
It was the first time they had
received the elements
from a woman.

    Some refused.
    Others were amused.
    A few wept.

What a breakthrough, Lord!
The old congregation

will never be the same.
It may never recover . . .

Six Months Later

Lord, the congregation recovered.
It was I who didn't!

Is it worth it?
I could live to be ninety-nine
and there will be those
who won't accept me—
or any woman.

How I worked for my ordination.
College and seminary were nothing
compared to the grilling I got
from the Board of Ministerial Standing.

And that is nothing compared
to what is happening now.

Lord, I'm lonely
scared
depressed
frustrated

and this is an awful way to live.
Lord, are all pioneers *martyrs*?
Or just me?

MAYBE THERE'S SOMETHING WRONG WITH ME

Maybe there's something wrong with me,
Lord, but I love power . . .

It all started when I took a job as
receptionist-secretary and screened
incoming clients who wished
to see the president . . .

Then I switched jobs and became an
acquisitions editor where the fate of
prospective writers rested
in the palm of my hand . . .

Now I'm working overseas in the consular
department. No one gets a visa unless
I approve (with few exceptions).

It's strange, Lord.

Something's happening to me.
My heart is turning from ice
into stone and I don't think
I like it
but I don't want to
surrender my power over others.

Today I refused a visa for a
young girl who wanted to be
nearer her fiancé. Sure, I went
by the book but I could have
easily granted a six-month visa
which would have made everyone

happy (even me) but I
   didn't because I
   wouldn't not because I
   couldn't . . .

Lord, help me do what is right
but while I'm doing it
remove this heart of stone
and give me more love for people
and less lust for power—
   if You would, please.

WHEN THREE IS A CROWD

My mother is a physician,
my father an osteopath . . .
both wanted me to become a dentist
but here I am—a chiropractor.

   You know, Lord, I'm not a rebel
   but our family is hopelessly divided—
   and for that I am deeply sorry.

It all began years ago when granny
was so ill we thought she would die.

   Mother couldn't help her.
   Nor father.
   But our neighbor did . . .
   a chiropractor.

That's when I decided to become a chiropractor.
Actually, I have more hours of medical
studies than either of my parents
but they still consider me a
"mickey mouse" doctor.

But that doesn't bother me, Lord.

During the years I have referred
many, many patients to physicians
and osteopaths—and to my parents.

But to this day they have not
referred one single patient to me.

I don't need the patients.
My days are too short as it is.

What bothers me is the simple fact
that there are some patients we
cannot help except to refer them
to someone who can.

Lord, I feel myself becoming
bitter and cynical at times
and my deepest prayer is that You
will not let it happen—not now or ever!

FIVE YEARS AND FIFTY POUNDS AGO

Remember, Lord, when I gave up
and quit trying to lose weight?
That was five years
and fifty pounds ago.
Hallelujah!

No, Lord, I don't mean to be
sacrilegious or disrespectful.
How I agonized and struggled
to peel those pounds off.
Now I've leveled at a jolly plateau

and I've never felt so good
in my whole life.

When I was trim—or skinny I
suppose I should say—I was
always on edge. Even worse, I was mean
when I was lean!

Today I come to work
and the kids love to
climb all over me
fighting to get their
good morning hugs.
I wouldn't trade this
for anything—especially
fifty blubbery pounds.

Sure, I know the chances of changing
from a *Miss* to a *Mrs.* have greatly
diminished—even though I'm more
lovable now than mean.

Oh, just one more thing, Lord.
If You don't really approve,
don't whisper in my ear.
Just stomp on my foot.
But don't forget that
I get mean when I'm lean!

A MATTER OF MORAL INTEGRITY

Ever since I was a teenager
I dreamed of being a lawyer.
Now I am one . . .

the pay is considerable
the hours are respectable
the score is unpredictable
(some I win, some I lose)

but now, Lord, I'm running into some snags.

Since my reputation is getting established,
I'm confronted with some extraordinary cases.
That's why I need Your guidance . . .
    more than ever!

    Expertise and strategies
    are no longer adequate.

    Now it's a matter of ethics
    and moral integrity
    as well as expertise and finesse.

At first I was preoccupied with winning—
at almost any cost—and I
trampled on my ideals in the process.

I made a lot of money but . . .

    Lord, I know pretty well what is
    right and wrong. The problem is
    changing my ego and operating
    on principle, not expediency.

Lord, I cannot play God . . .
I don't want to take over Your job!

    But do I take cases on a chronological
    or selective basis? Is it first come,
    first served, regardless . . . or must
    I choose on the basis of right and wrong?

Dare I represent only the underdog
or the guilty to atone for my biased past?

If You'll turn the pages, I'll start a new chapter.

A COMPUTER WITH A CONSCIENCE

As a computer programmer I am continually
amazed at the speed and accuracy
with which a computer
can work. It's
incredible!

Actually, Lord, it's only a human invention
but it's hardly human. Sometimes it's
actually inhuman.

It barks if we say, "Bark!"
It jumps if we say, "Jump!"
It sighs if we say, "Sigh!"

But if we make mistakes, it makes mistakes . . .
if we twist its tail, however, it won't bark.

No matter how we design it,
it's merely a mechanical wizard.

A wizard, yes!
A living wizard, no!

We are getting into all sorts of trouble now, Lord,
because we are building computers without a
conscience.

They collect enormous amounts of information
but they never forget a thing. Sometimes
they must forget but they cannot.

They have learned to manipulate people
but they are no respecters of persons
and they can and do turn against their masters.

Lord, my job is to make a computer
do what I tell it to do . . .
    no more, no less.

The trouble is—I can't do it.

How . . . I've got to know—
how can we give a computer
a conscience?

NUMBER PLEASE

Number please . . .
This is the operator.
What number are you calling?
I'm sorry, sir, no one by that name
is listed in the directory.
You are quite welcome.
Number please . . .

    Oh, excuse me, Lord.
    I must have dozed off
    as we were talking.
    I'm terribly sorry.

Why is it, Lord, that I would never
doze off while talking to anyone

under any circumstance but I
would do it to You?

    Is it because I can't see You?
    Is it because we talk only when
    I'm tired—or exhausted?
    Is it because I know You won't
    react negatively?

On the job I marvel at my patience—
and pleasantness, but I can be awfully
impolite with my roommates. Why?

    Why can't I always be the same?
    Why don't I scream at some of those
    awful people who make my job so
    miserable at times?
    Why do I spout off over matters
    so inconsequential at home?
    Why am I nice to people I abhor
    and mean to those I love?

Lord, I know You aren't finished
with me yet nor am I finished
with myself . . . but if it's possible,
would You give me just a little more grace
off the job as You have given me on it?

THE PERFECT JOB

Ah, yes, for awhile I thought
I had the perfect job.

I was a bit lazy
and tired of people.

Filling vending machines
is hardly a difficult task.
I make my rounds,
fill up the machines,
collect the coins
and call it a day.

Then, I expanded a bit and hired
a couple of helpers . . .

candy bars and peanuts
ballpoints and puzzles
kleenex and kotex
handkerchiefs and nail-clippers

Then we added a few more items:

cigars and cigarettes
comics and contraceptives

Before long I discovered a lucrative
market in girlie mags (the harmless kind)
and beer (nothing more than 3.4966) . . .

Finally I took a hotel franchise
and am supplying "corridorized" liquor
(they'd only go elsewhere anyway)
but I let my helpers handle this route.

Now I'm rolling in dough,
but I can't sleep too well nights.

That's why I thought I'd better
check with You, first, before
I go to a doctor.

You don't suppose I'm overdoing it,
do You?

FOR BETTER OR WORSE

Lord, remember how excited I was
when they pinned a cap on me?
    I couldn't eat or sleep
    for three days.

I'm right back there again, Lord,
but it's not because I'm excited.

This week I checked in daily
but I don't care if I never
check in again:
    two abortions
    six cases of VD
    four unwed mothers
    three cases of child abuse
    (two beatings, one malnutrition)
    one gunshot wound (domestic quarrel)
    five teenagers battered beyond recognition
    (drunken driving, all minors) . . .

I'm only a nurse, Lord,
but so many want me to play God.
Just today an attractive woman
queried me subtly on how to
put her aged mother to sleep—
    "gently but permanently"
    was the way she put it.

What do I do, Lord?
Must I spend my whole life
picking up the pieces and

mending the unmendable?
Why can't I practice preventative medicine?
Must I put my conscience to sleep?
Dare I put my faith into neutral?
Will my job go from bad to worse?

Oh, forgive me, Lord. It was a tough week.
Whatever, I now know I don't want Your job.
But I do want Your presence.

THE EXTORTIONIST

I must confess that my work
is getting distasteful . . .
and it's about time, isn't it?

We find a singer with some talent
and lots of saleable appeal . . .

recreate the image and assign
a promotable name . . .

Then we use and abuse the mass media
and sell him or her like we would
any other commodity.

When we're through—or they fade out—
we start with another all over again.

The public can be manipulated
and we extort as much as possible.

Now, Lord, it's starting to get to me.
I rather think that's because of You, since You
have impressed on me over and over again

that people are made in Your image
and are not to be exploited.

You did Your work well, Lord,
although it's taken a while with me.

We discovered a charming vocalist
at the *Club Erotika* and decided she
was a great possibility. But
something happened!

We fell in love. I'm taking her out
of this business. Since then she has
become a Christian, which brought me
to my senses.

We're going back into PR work, Lord.
Together. Only this time
we're going to work for You!

THE JUNK DEALER

I've been tossing and turning for hours.
I just can't sleep and I suppose
You know why, don't You?

These have been lean days.

Interest rates have gone up again.
The economy is sluggish.
People are saving,
not spending.

But people must live.
Transfers are being made.
Houses are being sold.

Even so, I knew better, Lord.

I sold a piece of junk
and now I'm paying for it.

I don't understand it . . .
I've never done this before.

    I knew the area floods easily.
    I knew the electrical system was borderline.
    I knew the prevailing winds were bad.
    I knew about the crack in the foundation
      but I said nothing.
      The sale was more important.

Now I have money in the bank
but my soul has declared bankruptcy.

Lord, it's not always easy
representing both buyer and seller
but that's why I have enjoyed
real estate—until now.

This time I misrepresented both
buyer and seller—and
the realtor.

Guess I didn't make much of a
commission today,
did I?

SIMPLE SURGERY . . .

Why must a surgeon be human?
Wouldn't it be easier

to simply be a
specialist?

I have little trouble at the
operating table or in making the
rounds among the convalescents.

Isn't that enough, Lord?

It would sure simplify matters
if someone else made the
diagnosis and prognosis
and another followed through
after surgery and immediate convalescence.

Then I could do what I love to do
and what I am best prepared to do.

But, no! It doesn't work that way.

Mrs. J was back in again today.
I'm quite sure her cancer is inoperable
but how do I tell her? Today she couldn't
find a baby sitter and brought her
toddler with her. Lord, I honestly can't bear
the thought of those big brown eyes
without a mama . . . but I'm
afraid that's going to be.

Ms. K was back in again today, too.
Wants another abortion.
Last time I refused and she sued.
Now she's back again.

Lord, my emotions have been shredded today.
Why can't I be a simple surgeon and merely
do simple surgery . . . ?

I suppose it's because life isn't quite that simple.
You'll forgive me for feeling this way, won't You?

Tomorrow I'll try hard to be an unsimple surgeon.

THE DIRT ON MY GREEN THUMB

Lord, maybe it's a good thing
I flunked out of college.
It's taken a few years to realize this
but now I'm glad. Very glad.

   I had dreamed of becoming a
   landscape architect and
   tree surgeon but here I am:
   a gardener and tree-trimmer.

Maybe the lack of a degree
made a better man out of me.

After my early morning cup of coffee
and a few moments with You,
I can hardly wait until I get
into the greenhouse to see
how my family is doing.

   Am I crazy because I love my work?
   Am I eccentric because I talk to the plants?
   Am I selfish because I guard against amateurs?

You know our gardens took first place
in a contest we didn't even enter.
I am pleased because I know You are pleased.

   I can plant a bulb but I can't make it grow
   I can select a color but I can't create it

I can pray for rain but I can't answer my own
   prayers

Lord, I feel so close to You
out here in Your garden.
I simply want to thank You for
letting me take care of Your
flowers and trim Your trees.

I also want to thank You
for the dirt on my green thumb.

Without it I would be nothing.